THE ?! LITTLE BOOK OF ICK

ANNA BURTT & KITTY WINKS

THE ?!
LITTLE
BOOK
OF
ICK

500 REASONS TO GET
OVER THEM - FOR GOOD

Laurence King Publishing

Contents

Welcome to

The Little Book of Ick

Now, you may already be an Ickspert, totally up with the idea of The Ick and wanting help using it to get over that heinous ex, or you may be looking for an insight (Icksight?) into this cultural phenomenon. Whatever the case, thanks for coming. Strap in, it might get weird.

What is The Ick?

It's that low-level feeling of dread and repulsion that you get when the person you're seeing does something – often completely harmless – that repulses you. From that point forward you are repelled by them. It triggers a physical response that is often felt in the pit of the stomach or the throat, and will render things forever changed between the two of you. In our research, we've found that The Ick is a physical manifestation of a gut feeling that may have been lying dormant. It's your body's way of waving a red flag to tell you that this person is not the one. You may well find your significant other 'icky', but this is different. There's no coming back from getting The Ick.

In recent years people have used The Ick to their advantage, to help them get over an ex or stop fancying someone unsuitable. For instance: imagine that toxic person you're completely obsessed with licking Nutella off every individual finger, or talking about themselves in the third person. See? It worked, didn't it?

So why do you need this book? Because it'll help to validate those uncontrollable feelings of repulsion when you go off someone; it'll help you get over your ex; you'll have a laugh along the way; and we guarantee you'll get that light-bulb moment when you realize: yes, that's what that was – I had The Ick! The ideas in this book have been tried and tested and we are confident they will help you get over that ex you just can't shift (or dump them if you know you need to). Even if you didn't get The Ick for them during your time together, imagining them in these Ick-inducing scenarios is bound to kick them out from living rent-free in your head. Remember all the things they did that made you feel Icked out ... pasta sauce round their mouths ... calling themselves a mixologist when they made a mojito once ... Think of all the things you don't have to witness now you're not with them, and breathe a sigh of relief. Use this book as a tool to return to when writing your lists of pros and cons about an ex, or a soon-to-be ex.

In *The Little Book of Ick* we cover the life cycle of the modern relationship, from initial (often online) behaviour to that first date, to spending more time together, to living together, taking holidays and more. We also treat you to some deliciously awful Ick anecdotes that have been submitted to us. We've kept these anonymous, because these Icks speak for themselves (and because we didn't want any exes flexing their lawsuit muscles).

Now, a disclaimer. Before some of you get upset that we're awful, judgemental people, we must state that:

1. **We do loads of these Icks all the time. No one is Icksempt from being Ick-inducing.**
2. **We're not judging anyone. The Ick defies logic and judgement.**
3. **We're trying to help you get over people – you'll thank us later.**
4. **We're validating some of your strangest thoughts.**
5. **It's not that deep.**

One thing we've learned is how bonding it is to discuss with friends the things that really repulse us, whether they make sense or are completely random. We've found out things we'd never have known otherwise, and admitted to feelings we always felt ashamed about. In this book we've included a few Ick-based games for you to play with your mates so that you can experience some of the hilarity and joy that we did putting this together.

Before you dive in, be warned: once you know, you know. You'll start noticing Icks at every turn. Once you get The Ick, there is no going back.*

*We'd like to think that true love is when you love someone in spite of the things that give you The Ick. If you're lucky, you'll find their toothpaste chin endearing rather than repellent.

Swipes and Gripes

The internet has transformed the way we date, mate and hate. It's fertile ground for breeding dicks and Icks. Behind the safety of a screen, we all feel that bit more confident, that bit more bolshy, and things can get that bit more bizarre. We've done a deep dive into the tech-related and online behaviour that makes your stomach turn. From selfies to Spotify, we'll be shocked if you don't recognize at least one here.

1
Recording
themselves
playing the guitar

THE LITTLE BOOK OF ICK

2
Googling the lyrics to
a rap so they can nail it
at the next party

3
Googling
'inspirational quotes'

4
Never acknowledging
it when you react to
their Stories

5
Searching on Urban
Dictionary for something
a friend said

6
The second link being
their SoundCloud when
you Google their name

7
Recording
a YouTube tutorial

8
Using a video tutorial
to relace their shoes

9
Thinking about what
to write on their dating
app bio and typing it out

10
Sending the sad face emoji
when you don't respond
within five minutes

11
Using the monkey
emojis unironically

12
Starting a social
media post with
'Some personal news'

13
Having a Pinterest board
for *Animal Crossing*
island design ideas

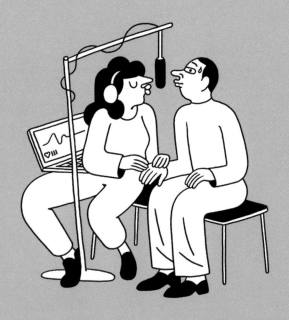

16

Liking a bikini pic on Instagram

'It's so common, and of course lots of people have no issue with it, but I immediately picture them hunched over a phone or laptop in a dark room and nothing turns me off quicker, doesn't matter how long ago it was. With girls it's just like "Aw that's sweet, she's supporting Megan Fox's underwear endeavours." With a bloke it's like absolutely not.

My ex-boyfriend liked a photo of a celebrity reclining on her kitchen counter in her underwear while we were together, and when I saw it I was like "Oh, that might actually have dried me out forever ...."'

17

Learning a TikTok dance,
getting annoyed with
themselves when they
mess up a move and
having to start again

18
When they react
to every one of your
Stories without fail

19
Scrolling through
their camera roll to
choose the perfect
dating app pictures

20
Over- or unnecessary
use of the cry/laugh
emoji

21
Offering unsolicited
feedback under people's
social media posts

22
Asking in earnest
if you use Snapchat

23
Listing 'the sesh'
as a hobby

24
Spending ages searching
for the right emoji

25
Picking out their
phone wallpaper

26
Picking out a phone case

27
Watching an ad for
a phone game and then
downloading the game

28
Sitting watching music
videos on YouTube

29
Waiting for the Spotify
ad to finish before
showing you a song

30
Recording themselves
to see if they can sing

31
Asking if you're
on social media

32
Singing in a voicenote

33
Doing a fake sexy
laugh on a voicenote

34
Teaching themselves
how to hula hoop from
an online tutorial and
getting really frustrated

35
Standing for half
an hour in silence
taking selfies

36
Announcing anything
online by saying
'I did a thing'

37
Sliding into someone's
DMs and the last
message on the thread
is when you blanked
them last time

38
DMing a celebrity to
tell them how much they
love/respect them

39
Rewatching their
Instagram Story before
posting it

40
Tagging a company
in a photo of clothes
they paid for

41
Commenting with the
heart-eye emoji under
an influencer's photo

42
Posting regularly in
Facebook community
groups

45
Unironically sticking
their tongue out
in a dating
app photo

43
Trying to think of their
Instagram caption

44
Overenthusiastic
texting

*'I had a girlfriend who
whenever she found
something funny over
text would message
"Hahahahahaa!"
The exclamation
mark put me off her
when I'd actually
really fancied
her before.'*

46

Listing their spirit animal on their dating app bio

47
Starting an Instagram
Live and making
awkward small talk
while they wait for the
other person to join

48
Replying to a celebrity's
tweets as if they
know them

49
Uploading the
recipe to their dinner
that absolutely no one
asked for

50
Writing an Instagram
caption pretending
to be their pet

51
Being really upset
when their tattoo artist
doesn't post a photo of
their tattoo

52
Having a week's
all-inclusive holiday
and adding 'travel'
to their bio

53
Talking like an
influencer on
their Stories

54
Entering an
Instagram competition
and posting it all
over their Stories

55
*'A guy used too many
hyphens when he texted.*

*I felt like I was texting
my dad.'*

56
Referring to
their 'knickers'
when sexting

THE LITTLE BOOK OF ICK

58

Sending you
a nude pic with
stuffed toys in
the background

THE LITTLE BOOK OF ICK

59
Adding 'mixologist' to their bio because they watched a tutorial for three different cocktails

60
Replying to a message with a video of themselves

61
Uploading videos of themselves lip-synching

62
Keeping a list on their phone of everyone they've slept with

'Someone once invited me over, made us cocktails, cooked us a four-course meal, all delicious, then when we were in his room cuddling on his bed he showed me a note on his phone with a list of every person he had ever slept with.

He said he wanted to "remember them".

I wanted to forget it ever happened.

I left five minutes later.'

63
Posing for a solo photo and not knowing what to do with their arms

64
Saying 'hey you'

65
Setting up a self-timer photo

66
Asking a brand for a discount because of their online following and being told no

Meeting and Deleting

Have you ever been totally obsessed with someone before you meet, only to go on a date and be repulsed by the smallest, most mundane thing they do? You are not alone.

Many of us will have been put off by photos of blokes with fish they've caught, or with their grandma or dog, to make them look more wholesome ... but what happens when you do meet? We spoke to hundreds of shes, hes and theys about their dating experiences and what has truly made their stomachs turn. From messy eaters to telling you about their stocks and shares, you'll find something here to make you squirm in recognition.

67
Ordering from
the kids' menu

68
Doing small blows
on a spoon to cool
the food down

69
Eating something
too hot and doing
the frantic breathing/
hand-fanning

70
Having to spit out
food that's too hot
into their serviette
and then fold it over

71
Ordering milk
at a Mexican
because they're
struggling with the
medium-hot

72
Cutting up their spaghetti

73
Asking for ketchup at
an Italian restaurant

74
Struggling to open
a tiny sauce sachet

75
Pushing their vegetables
to the side of their plate

76
Cutting up their food
into tiny chunks

77
Saying 'I'm not really
a dessert person'

78
Holding a tray of
food at a buffet

79
Taking a retainer out
to eat

80
Thinking they're the
main character
wherever they are

*'I once met a guy
online who was waiting
for me at a bar wearing
horn-rimmed glasses,
with one foot on a
chair, swirling brandy
around a glass like he
was plucked from a
bad 1980s porno.*

*I'd love to say it was
ironic, but alas.*

*Needless to say,
it was Ick at first sight.'*

81
Catching your eye
from ages away and
having awkward eye
contact while they're
walking towards you

82
Asking you where
the bathroom is as
soon as you arrive in
a restaurant, despite
the fact that neither
of you have ever
been before

83
Ordering something
from a menu, finding
out the restaurant
doesn't have it, then
getting huffy and
saying, 'I was really
looking forward to that'

Eating with their hands and their fingers go fully into their mouth

THE LITTLE BOOK OF ICK

85
Folding their arms
when looking at a menu

87

Licking the side of a wine glass

'I went on a wine-tasting date and the guy kept licking the drips down the side of the glass.

I'm not even sure how the wine got there, but I could see his tongue through the glass.'

88
Not being able to get
the server's attention

89
Holding a slice of pizza
and getting frustrated
when it starts flopping

90
Shouting 'Woo' when
a bottle of bubbles
is opened

91
Licking every finger
at the end of a meal

92
Tentatively licking
the food on their
spoon to see if it's
cool enough to eat

93
Eating an olive, not
realizing it has a pit and
getting a bit shocked

94
Asking for the
wine list in a chain
restaurant

95
Holding their cup
with both hands

96
Picking food out
of their teeth and
then eating it

97
Trying to squeeze out
of a booth doing the
exaggerated comedy
breathe-in and
mini-shuffle combo

98
Taking away their
leftover food in
a Tupperware and
walking around
withit for the rest
of the evening

99
Walking with confidence
into a pub, only to get
turned away for being
too drunk

100
Making a Boomerang
of their cocktails

101
Calling wine 'vino'

102
Only drinking craft beer

103
Holding on to their straw
while drinking out of it

104
Missing the straw
with their mouth

105
Accidentally biting
their cutlery

106
Choking on water and
going red in the face

107
Pretending their
drink hasn't missed
their mouth and subtly
trying to wipe away
the dribble

108
Saying 'I'll have what
they're having' and
then being disappointed
when it arrives

109
Sitting on a bar stool and
having to swing their legs

110
*'I was seeing a guy
with a beard and he
took a sip of his beer
and had loads of foam
in his moustache.'*

112
Spitting as they speak, leaving a little spit bubble sitting on the table between you so that you both have to pretend it's not there

113
Jumping up and down to music with their hands in the air

114
Mistiming a beat drop

115
Intensely breakdancing

116
Tottering in heels and trying to play it off

117
Buying merch at a gig and putting it on immediately

118
Trying really hard to get into the middle of a mosh pit and failing, having to stand on the edge

119
Getting into the middle of a mosh pit and being thrown around like a scarecrow

120
Taking a video of themselves at a concert

121
Getting strapped into a rollercoaster

122
Really enjoying a rollercoaster

123
Walking up to bowl in a bowling alley

124
Standing aimlessly
watching the bowling
ball after a release

125
Really stomping
on a dance mat

126
Getting really excited
about a photo booth

127
Cradling their popcorn
trying to find a seat in
the cinema

128
Trying to disguise the fact
they have finished all the
popcorn before the movie
has started

129
Saying 'Ooooh, a really
good bit is coming up'
when watching a movie

130
Going to pour
a glass of wine but
finding there's nothing
left in the bottle

131
Going to pour
a glass of wine
without realizing
the lid is still on

132
*'One (English) guy
said "Dat ASSSSSSSS"
in an American
accent as I bent over
in front of him.'*

133
Drinking out of
a little carton

134
Walking fast towards
an empty seat, only for
someone to sit down in it
before they can get there

Getting BDSM and ASMR confused

136
Clapping when a movie
ends in the cinema

137
Googling the plot of a
movie right after seeing it

138
Having to cling on
to the side while ice
skating and watching
all the kids pass

139
Eating a Happy Meal
as an adult

140
Finishing choking on
their food but still having
that little lingering cough
they're trying to cover up

141
Asking if you're
a good kisser

142
Pulling away
from kissing with
their fake eyelash
hanging off

143
Repeatedly asking
what your type is,
hoping you'll
describe them

144
Thinking they're
Bear Grylls because
they remembered
a portable charger

145
Saying their
mom or dad is their
best friend

146
Changing their
voice depending
on who they're with

147
Quietly singing along
to a song in the secret
hope you'll tell them
how good they are

148
Nonchalantly trying
to show off their new
tattoo in the hope
you'll ask about it

149
Unironically winking

150
Asking the cab
driver if they're having
a busy night

151
Having a bit of saliva
on their lip that
attaches to the other
lip as they talk

152
Asking for
a cuddle

153
Talking in the
third person

154
Using a chef's
kiss gesture
unironically

155
Using a Velcro
wallet

156
Sucking their finger
to get lipstick off
their teeth

157
Talking about
'their industry'

158

Being completely convinced their pub quiz answer is correct, and when it's not, spending the rest of the night justifying why they thought it was

159

Their sweat dripping into your mouth when they're on top

160

Having a sulk about wearing a condom

161
Having their wallet
on a chain

Attempting to get up
from a bean bag

163

*'Went on a date with
a girl, ended with a snog
at the train station,
all going well until she
started making "umhhh"
"ahhh" noises into
my mouth.*

It was so bizarre.

*Block, delete, ignore,
forget.'*

164

Pretending they
didn't hear the
slurping noise when
the condom comes off

165

Personifying
their genitalia

166

Asking how it was
for you after sex

167

*'There's nothing
less sexy than
when you're trying
to get down to business
and you both keep
tumbling into the
crevice of doom
created by being
too lazy to flip
your mattress.'*

168
Keeping their socks
on during sex

Making it Public

So you've been dating for a while, you've soft-launched them online, you've told your friends and your date may even have met your family.

You're starting to spend more time in each other's everyday lives, which may not be as sexy as you envisaged.

You've realized that they don't wake up before eleven at the weekend, that they trip over every uneven surface and absolutely love it when people sing 'Happy Birthday' in restaurants.

Walking with
an umbrella
and it blowing
inside out

170
Kicking a football
in a park to show off,
and missing it

171
Wearing a Lycra
cycling unitard

172
Riding an
electric scooter

173
Having a mini-fall
off an electric
scooter, getting
back on and looking
round to make sure
no one saw

174
Walking down the
street with their
music blasting out
of a speaker

175
Trying to pass a stranger
on the street and
going the same way
more than once

176
Putting their hand
out for a cab and it
driving past

177
Doing the mini-jog to
catch up with someone

178
Trying to overtake
someone on the street
but not being able to
out-walk them and having
to walk side by side

179
Walking down a hill and
having to do the little
shuffle walk, leaning back
to keep their balance

180
Having to walk on
the grass because
there isn't enough
room on the street

181
Saying 'brekkie'

182
Waving at someone
and getting blanked

183
Purposefully making
their ponytail swing
when they walk

184
Thinking someone
is waving at them
but it's actually at the
person behind

185
Being splashed
by a passing car

186
Doing the little
walk up and down
when trying shoes
on in a store

187
Holding clothes up
to themselves in
a store mirror

188
Getting changed
in a fitting room and
coming out and doing
the little fashion show

189
Winning a raffle

190
Saying 'expresso'

191
Asking a barista
to remake
their drink

THE LITTLE BOOK OF ICK

192

Falling in front of a group and being like 'I'm good, I'm good'

193

Keeping their earbuds in no matter what they're doing

194
Having a preferred
country of origin for
their coffee beans

195
Asking a barista
what syrups they have

196
*'Whenever he had
his arm around me,
he would use his nose
to open notifications
on his Apple watch.*

*It made me cringe
so much I couldn't
even look.'*

197
Stalling the car and trying
to play it off

198
Walking confidently to
the top deck of the bus,
finding that it's full and

having to sheepishly
walk back downstairs

199
Losing their balance on a
bus while trying to get off

200
Running for a bus while
it drives off and having
to play it off

201
Eating something in public
and there's no rubbish bin
so having to walk around
holding the wrapper

202
Trying to be cocky
crossing the street but
having to jump back on
to the street because
the lights changed

203
Wearing fingerless
gloves

204
Getting really stressed
and upset when trying
to parallel park

205
Ordering a mocha

206
Telling people about
their Groupon deals

207
Getting yelled at
publicly for being in
the wrong line

208
Messing up the
self-checkout and
having to get someone
to come and help

209
Checking themselves
out in a store window

210
Waiting their turn
to hold the bottle
of liquor for a photo

211
Not being able to keep
up with the cashier and
having a panic trying
to throw everything
into their bag

212
Tripping over the cart
wheel in a supermarket

213
*'When their sock slips
into their shoe and they
try to find it and pull it up
while still walking.'*

214
Doing the little run
across the street when
a car lets them cross

THE LITTLE BOOK OF ICK

215
Having 'Happy Birthday'
sung to them in public

216
Singing 'Happy Birthday'
to someone in public

217
Doing the Cha-Cha Slide

218
Saying 'Woah, slow down there, speed racer' when you're driving

219
Doing parkour in public

220
Doing parkour anywhere

221
Spontaneous rapping

222
Chanting 'Girls' night' when doing shots on a night out

223
Asking the DJ if they can hop up and show some of the mixes they've made

224
Clapping in any form

225
Having strong opinions about whether jam or cream should go first on a scone

226
Getting up prematurely when the train is nearing the stop and having to stand around aimlessly

227
Thinking a cashier is free, walking forward and then having to walk back into the line when it turns out the cashier is serving someone else

228
Jumping into a dance circle and doing the Chicken Dance with zero hesitation

229
Being handed the AUX at a party and looking round to make sure everyone is listening

230
Pronouncing 'paella' and 'chorizo' as if they're from Spain

231
Using a reusable water bottle and the mouth bit being all chewed up

232
Pulling out a guitar at a party and everyone trying to avoid their area

233
Trying to lean forward in the car but the seatbelt jolting and having to try again slowly

234
Covering their ears when a train passes

Their ass sticking out
of a medical gown

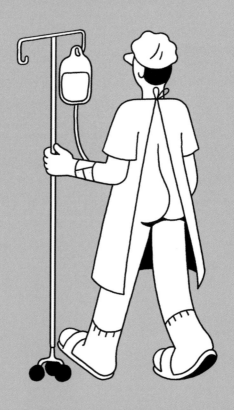

Taking their shirt off
the minute they
consume any liquor

237
Shouting 'WEEE'
as they go down
steep hills or over
speed bumps

238
Leaping over
a puddle while
out on a run

239
Trying to start
a Mexican wave and
it not catching on

240
Running up to
a bird to scare it,
and it not moving

THE LITTLE BOOK OF ICK

241
Wearing a festival
wristband for months
after it ends

242
Wearing the big
optician glasses

243
Starting to sing with
total confidence and
it being a remix

244
Throwing confetti
right at the bride
and groom rather
than over them gently

245
Being slowly reclined
in a dentist's chair

246
Owning a hankie and
washing it *slightly* less
often than they should

247
Bouncing in
a car going over
speed bumps

248
Crowd-surfing

249
Shaking a vending
machine with an
increasing level
of frenetic energy
because it hasn't
released their snack

250
Being spun around
in a hairdresser's chair

251
Trying to use
a gift card and
being told there's
no money on it

252
Smelling a candle
in a store and having
an aggressive reaction
when they don't like
the scent

253
Sitting in the back
of the car and trying
to stay involved in
the conversation
when they clearly
can't hear anything

254
Pulling in too far at
the drive-thru and having
to do a tiny reverse

255
Getting annoyed if you
get *anything* on their car

256
Really grinning
when sledding

257
Doing the little duck
when a bird flies in
front of them

258
*'He tried to give money
to a random hipster
rolling a cigarette
because he thought
he was homeless.'*

259
Spitting out their
gum and it missing
the rubbish bin

260
Waving to a driver for
letting them pass, but it
was just a stop light

261
Throwing away their gum,
not quite getting it all out
of their mouth and having
the leftover stringy bit

THE LITTLE BOOK OF ICK

262
Trying to lift a weight
that's too heavy
and attempting to
play it off with their
face scrunched up

Skipping

264
Hearing a squeaky
shoe in public and
immediately shouting
'Who farted?'

265
Owning a pogo stick

266
Falling off a pogo stick

267
Jumping up and down
on the spot when they
don't get their way

268
Yelling 'Bingo!'

269
Asking a store
assistant for help
and they don't hear

270
Enthusiastically
doing the New Year's
countdown

271
Watching themselves in
the mirror lifting weights

272
Walking up to automatic
doors and they don't
open so having to walk
back and try again

273
Trying to merge on
the freeway and not
being let in

274
Wearing a band
T-shirt and hoping
everyone notices

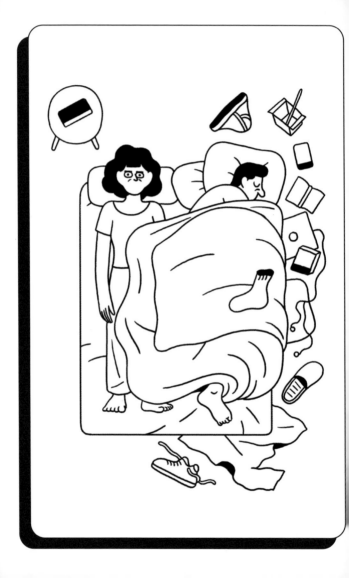

Too Close for Comfort

Let's face it, when the veil is dropped, we all let ourselves go a bit. No judgement there.

But the intensity that comes with cohabitation also brings a lot of Icks to the surface.

Until now you may have got away with not knowing what someone does in the shower, or what they do as soon as they get home from work.

There's no hiding when you live together, and our research showed that many very much 'in love' couples had no idea what they were embarking on when they decided to live under the same roof.

Lying in bed in the foetal position

276
Accidentally scratching
you with their toenails
in bed

277
Their fingernail trimmings
pinging across the room

278
Putting on a fitted sheet
and it keeps popping off

279
When they get dressed
from the top down and
their genitals hang out

280
Owning a dreamcatcher

281
Having a favourite pillow

282
Putting their socks on
before anything else

283
Calling themselves
a 'plant parent'

284
Tying the little bow
on their pyjama pants

285
Struggling to pull out
a sofa bed

286
Neatly folding and
laying out their clothes
for the next day

287
Taking the trash out
in flip-flops

288
Taking the recycling out,
finding that the bins
are full and having
to walk back sheepishly
carrying it

Wearing slippers

290
Cutting the crusts off
their sandwiches

291
Carrying on singing
even though the music
has gone off

292
*'My first husband, when
poorly, asked me to
make his childhood soup,
so I called my mother-
in-law (a sweet, lovely
woman, but possibly the
world's worst cook) and
asked her about it.*

*It was a portion of coley,
that grey, smelly fish that
people buy for their cats,
boiled for 30 mins in two
cans of tomato soup.*

*Husband made it (with
a great deal of sniffing
and coughing and*

*resentful stares) and
ate the whole thing.'*

293
Trying really hard to
peel an orange without
breaking the skin

294
Picking out bits of food
from the sink drain

295
Eating a lollipop

296
Accidentally grating
their finger

297
Wearing oven mitts

298
Wearing an apron
to cook

299
Using the word 'tummy'

300
Doing the little jump
to pull their trousers up

303
Putting a dish towel
over their shoulder
when cooking

304
Describing salt
as seasoning

305
Trying to carry too
many bags of shopping
from the car and having
to power-walk so they
don't drop them

306
Pretending not
to see when the
cookies are being
passed around,
then acting surprised
when they are offered

307
Having a favourite
dish towel

308
Being unable to eat
a banana without
deep-throating it
and thinking they're
a comedy genius

309
Packing a lunch box
for work

310
Licking the inside of
a yoghurt-pot lid

311
Having shelves with
trophies on, or a money
box shaped like a football

312
Closing the fridge door
with their hip

313
Laughing and saying
'Give it five' after
leaving the toilet

314
Insisting on following
recipes to the letter and
getting really stressed
when this isn't possible

315
Refilling the ice-cube tray

316
Struggling to get ice out
of an ice-cube tray

317
Having a favourite mug

318
Crushing a can with
their hand

319
Consulting the little
sheet when picking
a chocolate from the box

320
Sticking their toothbrush
too far down and gagging

321
Cleaning their
toothbrush

322
Standing on tiptoes
to reach something
high up, then having
to relaunch themselves
when they can't
quite reach

323
Hacking into the sink

324
Using shampoo
to wash their face

325
Dropping a bath
bomb in and standing
there watching it fizz

326
Having toothpaste
crust around
their lips

THE LITTLE BOOK OF ICK

327
Throwing
a controller
in frustration

328
Having to sheepishly
pick up a controller
again to play

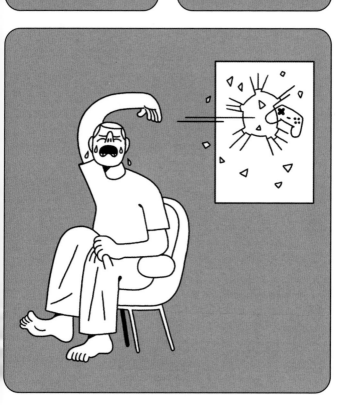

329
Clogging the razor
with their pubes

330
Personifying an
inanimate object, e.g

*'No need to slam
the door, what's it
done to you?'*

331
Putting milk in first
when making a cup of tea

332
Avidly polishing a glass

333
Really enjoying
putting on lip balm

334
Thrusting their penis
up and down really fast
when they get out of the
shower, then laughing

335
Neatly placing
a plaster over their cut

336
Leaving toothpaste
in the sink after
they've spat it out

337
Getting in the bathtub
and it's too hot so
trying to hop out again

338
Putting a towel round
their shoulders when they
come out of the shower

339
Standing aimlessly
buck naked in the
shower waiting for
the water to warm up

340
Aggressively washing
their butt crack

341
Lying on their
frontin the bath

342
Doing the little
dance when they
need the toilet but
someone is using it

343
Eating anything
straight out of
the can

344
Stroking their
stomach after eating

345
Giving themselves
a pep talk out loud
in the mirror

346
Screaming for
someone to bring
them more toilet roll

347
Their ass sticking
to a shower curtain

348
Picking out their hair
from the shower drain

349
Using a nasal spray and
being a bit taken aback
when the spray hits

350
Owning a Thermos

351
Wearing a towel hat

352
Slipping in the shower
and trying to hold on
to the water

353
Wearing the full bathrobe
and slippers combo

354
Sitting on the toilet with
their piece of toilet paper
neatly folded ready

355
Talking to Alexa and
she isn't understanding

357
Walking up the
stairs two at a time

356
Not knowing
what to do
when their dog
humps their leg

358
Walking up the
stairs on all fours

TOO CLOSE FOR COMFORT

359
Making sure
no one is looking,
then lifting up their
top when they walk
past a mirror to see
if they have abs

361
Getting a paper cut
and being really upset,
saying 'It really is
the worst pain'

362
Being so upset
they inadvertently
stomp

360
Licking an envelope
over-enthusiastically

THE LITTLE BOOK OF ICK

363
Gatekeeping
their Netflix password

364
Sharpening pencils

365
Licking their fingers
when separating papers

366
Using a random object
to scrape dirt from
under their nails

367
Taking issue with
an inanimate object

368
Wheeling across the
room in a wheelie chair

369
Leaning too far back in
their chair but not falling,
just having that huge
jolt and a little yelp

370
Chasing after something
with grabby hands

371
Grabby hands

372
Tweeting a radio station

373
Saying 'fur babies'
when referring to
their pets

374
Saying 'We've been busy'
when announcing
a pregnancy*

*Sorry – we know you
probably don't want to
get The Ick at this stage,
but it's the truth!*

Sun, Sea and See Ya Later

Trips with lovers are funny, aren't they?

Out of your usual routine, on neutral territory, in a different country ... what could possibly give you The Ick? Well, a lot, it seems.

Turns out that airports, planes, strange currency and even buffets can bring on The Ick.

And, really, as much as we deny it, flip-flops are kinda weird.

Especially when they're paired with blue jeans and a fancy fedora.

375
Counting down
'sleeps'

376
Saying 'holibobs'
instead of 'holiday'

377
Practising packing
to make sure it all
fits and is the
right weight

378
Having a holiday
folder with all the
documents ready

379
Wheeling a suitcase
down the street,
it flipping over, and
having to sheepishly
stop to turn it back
round and carry on

380
Running through
the airport with
a wheelie suitcase

381
Running with
a rucksack on

382
Reading an entire
in-flight magazine
while trying to look
genuinely engaged

383
Paying *full* attention
to the in-flight
safety demonstration
and repeatedly
looking to check
that you are too

384
Clapping when
the plane lands

386
Taking loads of
photos of the rental
car before driving
it away

387
Using mini hair
straighteners

388
Realizing they've
taken a wrong turn,
so just standing and
looking at their phone
trying to play it off

389
Having to mop their
forehead with a little
towel because
they're so hot

390
Waiting for their toast
to finish in the buffet
toast machine

391
Saying 'Ahhhhhh'
when taking a sip
of cold water

392
Trying to find a spot at
the beach while carrying
all their things

393
Wobbling barefoot on
a pebble beach trying to
look like it doesn't hurt

394
Putting on loads
of sunscreen

395
Wearing a life vest

396
Wearing goggles

397
Wearing a swimming cap

THE LITTLE BOOK OF ICK

398
Walking up to a hotel buffet excitedly with a plate

399
Playing in the sand

400

'When I was travelling I met a guy who I had
a bit of a fling with for a few days.

We separated to continue our travels, and kept
in touch.

When I told him via text that I was going to
another country with two of my best girlfriends,
he promptly invited himself along.

I felt a bit weird about this, but thought it
was too late to say we didn't want him there.
As soon as I saw him again, looking all eager,
with his backpack, I got that dreaded feeling
in the pit of my stomach. I'd got The Ick.

I kept him at arm's length, and a week into the
trip, after he had definitely got the picture that
I wasn't interested, I decided to tell him that we
should go our separate ways.

The poor guy was so upset and ended up crying!
He had done nothing wrong except like me
enough to hop on a plane and intrude on a girls'
holiday, bless him! He has a wife and baby now,
so it all worked out for him in the end ....'

402
Getting out of the
water with their hair
plastered to their head

403
Purchasing flip-flops

404
Wearing water shoes

405
Toasting a marshmallow
around a campfire and
then burning their
mouth on it

406
Taking tiny licks of
an ice cream because
it's too cold

407
Sighing in ecstasy
in a sauna

408
Doggy paddling

409
Chasing a
ping-pong ball

410
Being thrown around
on a bucking bronco

411
Wiggling their toes
in sandals

412
*'I went to the beach with
a guy and he sat up and
he had a stone kind of
stuck on his back and it
just gave me The Ick.'*

413
Getting stuck
trying to climb
overa fence

414
Standing in line
waiting for a
water slide

415
Being really upset
when their ice cream
melts down their hand

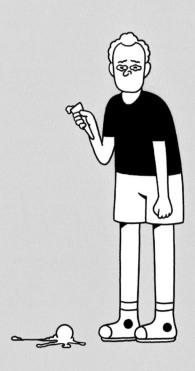

417
Going down
a water slide
with too
much glee

THE LITTLE BOOK OF ICK

418
Trying to speak the language but just speaking English with a really bad accent

419
Having absolute confidence in an accent they're doing

420
Trying and failing to haggle at a market

421
Licking a stamp and a bit of saliva trailing from their mouth to the stamp

422
Kissing a postcard before posting it

423
Having white smears of excess sunscreen

424
Bombing in the pool and looking around to see how big the splash was

425
Getting genuinely upset and sulking when they get pushed in a swimming pool

426
Getting upset about cabin bag allowances

427
Cling-filming hold luggage

428
Getting emotionally
involved with stray cats

Wearing an eye mask
on the plane

The Ugly Truth

So things have got serious, and you're seeing more of each other in your own spaces, spending more time at home on the sofa than dancing, eating out or taking romantic day trips.

Gone are the days when you lived in ignorance, imagining they were absolutely perfect behind closed doors, that those habits you hated weren't just one-offs, that they don't put their hand down their pants then smell it.

The more time we spend with people, the more we know them, the more we love them, *but* the higher the chance of catching The Ick.

From drinking instant soup to obsessing over a drone ... they say romance is dead; we just say it's unsustainable ...

430
Picking out
belly-button fluff

431
Picking their toes

432
Getting a jacket
zipper stuck and
flapping it about
trying to unjam it

433
Drinking a whole
glass of milk

434
Having an
unexpected nosebleed

435
Their flip-flops
slapping on the floor

436
Crying when their
team loses anything

437
Putting their
thumbs in their
jean pockets

438
Scratching
their crotch
and smelling it

439
Struggling to get
a hoodie over
their head

440
Googling the cast
of the TV show
they've just watched

441
Eating sliced fruit
from a packet

442
Trying to pop
a zit on an awkward
part of their body

443

Being pulled along by their dog

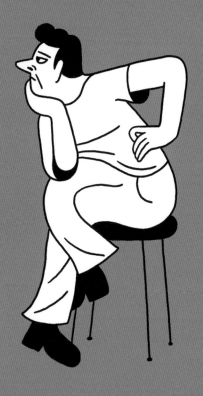

446
Pushing
a pull door

447
Calling their
mother 'mummy'

448
Saying 'the missus'

449
Saying 'the other half'

450
Saying 'the better half'

451
Using 'mum' as a verb

452
Singing incorrect
song lyrics with
absolute confidence

453
Saying 'circle back'

454
Having to repeat
the punchline of their
joke because no one
was listening

455
Dropping something
and it starts rolling so
having to do the little
run to catch it

456
Wearing a clip-on necktie

457
Punching the air

458
Saying 'nothink'
or 'somethink'

459
Saying 'vibe'

460
Saying 'muchly'

THE LITTLE BOOK OF ICK

462
Using 'magic' as an adjective

463
Sticking their tongue out in concentration

464
Approaching the dance floor too early during the first dance at a wedding and having to retreat into the crowd

465
Looking at the tissue after they have blown their nose

466
Making sure *everyone* knows the sacrifice they have made to be the designated driver

467
Trying to sneeze and it not coming out but still having the little sneeze face

468
Saying 'Bless me' when they sneeze

469
Covering their ears when an alarm goes off

470
Pretending they're not desperate to catch the bouquet at a wedding

471
Tipping up the chip packet to pour the crumbs into their mouth

472
Asking if you'd like them to come over and cook you dinner, then bringing a TV dinner

474
Finger guns

476
Saying 'methinks'

477
A stomping tantrum

478
Using a glue stick

479
'Trying out' a nickname

480
Pretending to be so deep in concentration that they don't hear you speak to them

481
Having to use hand gestures to remember left and right

482
Calling their parents by their first names

483
Having in-depth plans for their Oktoberfest trip

484
Saying 'arvo'

485
Saying 'coolio'

486
Being startled by a loud noise

487
Doing the thumbs up

488
Trying to get hair off their tongue

489
Doing the double thumbs up

THE LITTLE BOOK OF ICK

490
Walking with
their hands behind
their back

491
Playing air guitar

492
'One time, I was meeting
a girl for a seafront cycle
date and she tried to
do that thing where you
move your leg over the
bike while it's moving to
get off and it tipped over.
It was our last date.'

493
Not being able to
get rid of their hiccups

494
Making a fart noise
accidentally with
a part of their body

and continuing to
re-create the noise
to prove it wasn't
a real fart

495
Chasing a sheet
of paper as it
flies away

496
Wearing
sunglasses inside,
unironically

497
Wearing
a high school or
university
graduation hoodie

498
Asking
someone if they
want to feel
their bicep

118

ying a sweater round
heir waist or shoulders

A final note from the 'Icksperts'

Thank you for buying *The Little Book of Ick.* We hope you had as much fun reading it as we did writing it.

On a slightly more serious note, though, the idea for this book came when Kit was trying to get out of a toxic situation and was telling Anna how she was using Ick prompts on TikTok to detach herself.

Anna (who is a bit older and still can't spell TikTok correctly the first time around) was fascinated, and once she looked into it, she felt validated in her often bizarre relationship choices.

It made what can feel isolating and a bit uncomfortable funny.

And that's what this is, a bit of fun.

So thank you to those TikTok (or TickTock) trailblazers, to everyone on the internet for making us laugh, and to the absolute morons we've dated who have inspired so many of these Icks.

You're all wonderful and awful (as are we).

Games

Getting The Ick can be a hugely bonding experience. Not only can it validate some of our strangest, most irrational-seeming thoughts, but also it can teach you things about your friends that you'd never have known otherwise. We've designed some Ick-based games along the lines of party classics to get it all out there into the open.

Ick Sherlock Holmes

How well do you know your friends?

1. Cut or tear slips of paper and make sure everyone has at least four.
2. Write Icks from the book or from your own experience on to them. One Ick for each piece of paper.
3. Fold them up and put them in a bowl, then take turns to pick one out and guess whose Ick it is.
4. If someone guesses you correctly as the author of the Ick, they get a point and you have to tell the story behind it, warts and all. If they get it wrong, you can keep your Icky secret safe and everyone else gets a point. The winner is the person with the most points when the bowl is empty. They are the true Sherl-Ick Holmes ...

Ick Charades

1. Split into two teams and flip a coin to decide who goes first.
2. One person from the starting team should close their eyes and flick through this book, landing on a random page. They then have 30 seconds to act out an Ick from that page using only their body – no words or sounds – and their team members have to guess what it is.

3. If the team guess it correctly within the time limit, they get the point; if not, the other team can shout out the answer. The winning team is the first to twenty points.

Ick Salad Bowl

The Salad Bowl game consists of three rounds: the Describing round; the Wordless Acting round basically charades); and the One Word Only round. The idea is that the game speeds up and gets more intense as you become familiar with the Icks in the bowl.

1. Split into teams of at least two people.
2. Cut or tear slips of paper and distribute them so that each person has the same number (at least four each).
3. Everyone should write down one Ick on each piece of paper, then fold it and put them into a bowl in the middle. Don't worry if some are repeated, it's inevitable and makes an even more hysterical game.
4. Set a timer for 40 seconds.
5. Round 1 (Describing): Pull out a piece of paper and describe the Ick, without using any of the words on the paper, to the other members of your team. Every one that's guessed is a point; you get

one pass, and at the end of the 40 seconds put all the incorrectly guessed ones back in the bowl. Repeat with all teams until the bowl is empty.

5. Round 2 (Wordless Acting/Charades): Put all the Icks back in the bowl. Set the timer and repeat round 1, this time acting out the Icks. You lose a point every time you use words or sounds.

6. Round 3 (One Word Only): Put all the Icks back in the bowl. Set the timer and repeat round 2, this time using only one word to describe each Ick. Using more than one word docks you a point. The winning team is the one with the most points when the bowl is empty after all three rounds.

About the authors

Kitty Winks is one of Instagram's sassiest book bloggers, known for her brutally honest opinions and refusal to conform to the norm. Like many respectable Gen Zs, Kitty now works at a tech startup, after having previously worked as a bookseller and museum guide.

Anna Burtt has worked in publishing for almost a decade and is currently Head of Events at a global writing consultancy. She is the host of the Brighton Book Club on Radio Reverb and has run a successful writing group for the last four years. She's recently finished her first novel, which is set in Yorkshire and explores grief, sexuality, intergenerational friendships and drag.

Acknowledgements

To all our mates and everyone who sent in their icks anonymously: thank you for reliving your dating trauma for the greater good.

To all our past, present and future dalliances: don't worry, we're all disgusting here.

Thank you, Andrew Roff, for trusting us and being a champion of *The Little Book of Ick* from day one.

Thank you to the Laurence King team, especially Catherine Pitt, Florian Michelet, Dan Jackson and Yadira Da Trindade, for all your hard work on this project.

Thank you to Simon Landrein for your ick-ceptional illustrations.

Finally, thank you for buying *The Little Book of Ick*. Tell your friends!

LAURENCE KING

First published in Great Britain in 2022
by Laurence King Publishing
an imprint of The Orion Publishing Group Ltd
Carmelite House, 50 Victoria Embankment
London EC4Y 0DZ

An Hachette UK Company

10 9 8 7 6 5 4 3 2 1

A CIP catalogue record for this book is
available from the British Library.

ISBN 978 1 399 60321 8

Design by Florian Michelet & Dan Jackson

Origination by DL Imaging, UK
Printed in China by C&C Offset Printing Co. Ltd

Laurence King Publishing is committed to ethical
and sustainable production. We are proud participants
in the Book Chain Project®. bookchainproject.com

www.laurenceking.com
www.orionbooks.co.uk